A SHAGGY DOG'S

BOOK OF HOURS

D1303190

A SHAGGY DOG'S BOOK OF HOURS

ANN KOEHLER

CAPRA PRESS / SANTA BARBARA
1991

Designed by George Delmerico.

Printed by McNaughton & Gunn.

LIBRARY OF CONGRESS CATALOGING-IN-PUBLICATION DATA

Koehler, Ann, , 1962–
    A shaggy dog's book of hours / by Ann Koehler.
        p.   cm.
    ISBN 0-88496-326-8 : $7.95
    1. Dogs—Pictorial works.   2. Dogs—Humor.   I. Title.
SF430.K58   1991   91-9663
                                                       CIP
                                                        AC

Published by Capra Press
Box 2068, Santa Barbara, CA 93120

INTRODUCTION

She is known as Duchess not only because she lives in the lap of luxury but also for the streak of Russian Wolfhound that appears among a dozen other strains in her bloodstream. As an urban dog she harbors a multitude of forgivable idiosyncrasies such as chasing cats, eating straw hats and sleeping on the couch. These must be the dimmed reflexes of the splendid beast that once pursued leopards across the Steppes, gnawed the hindquarters of caribou and slept in icebound caves.

Duchess leads a very civilized and, in our estimation, uneventful life. A glob of ice cream on a sidewalk or a plunge in

the harbor can make her day. Yet to her, these events make life worth living. By day she keeps herself busy and sometimes romps with shepherds and dalmatians as though they were her peers. But she's really more of a people person and enjoys a turn in the family wagon. She has even been known to frequent bars where she can be urged to perform a creditable mime of Rex Harrison or dance a hind-legged jig. Above all

this, she values her sleep most of all and rarely rouses herself before nine. Although the ways of her ancestors are long gone, watching her run or growl in her dreams makes us wonder sometimes.

Ah, Duchess, she has a twinkle in her eye, a wry wit and nary a mean bone in her body. If only she could talk, or at least keep a diary. Curiosity got the better of us. We loaded a camera and followed her one day and this is the tale that unfolded . . .

9:15

Time to rise and shine!

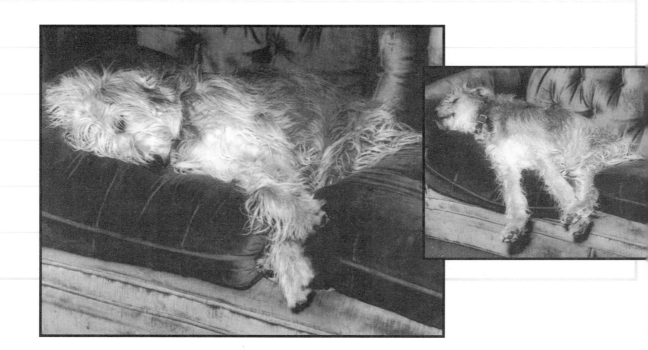

9:30

Me bleary?

One eye at
a time.

9:45

Up and at 'em...

9:55

...that's me!

I'm not
so good at
omelettes.

10:15

What's up?

Depends upon where you sit, looking in or looking out.

T'ai chi chuan
on the lawn.

10:45

They gave me a hat.

It just wasn't me, so I ate it.

11:00

It fell and broke all by itself.

But they'll never believe me...

...so I make myself scarce.

A spin in the family
wagon is always welcome.

11:25

11:30

Bus bench
a la mode.

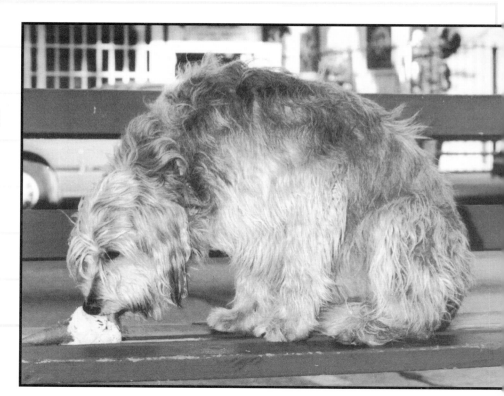

Mopping up,
as they say.

11:46

Sometimes it's not easy to live up to expectations.

12:00

Ducks make it look easy. But when I take to water I only get...

12:05

...drenched.

It's all becoming quite clear...

...I'm a
landlubber
at heart.

One of my

favorite

pursuits.

I know a few cats in high places.

Balls, hoops and hurdles whet a busy dog's appetite for whatever is put before her...

... even
if it's
pizza...

3:00

... or home-made cookies...

... or a nice little cupcake!

3:20

Ah, there's no place like home.

Naptime with Raggedy.

Look who's calling who what!

Then there's the bozo next door...

5:00

Boogeying with
Shep to the
juke box.

5:15

We're just
a coupla
party animals.

A rendezvous

with the true prince

in my life.

Therein hangs a tail.

Ann Koehler and her shaggy dog, Duchess, live in Santa Ana Heights, California, and run a photography studio well-known thoughout Orange County.